The Mindful Writer

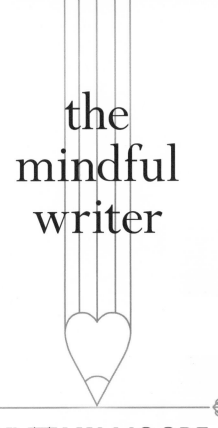

the mindful writer

DINTY W. MOORE

Wisdom

Wisdom Publications
199 Elm Street
Somerville MA 02144 USA
wisdompubs.org

Library of Congress Cataloging-in-Publication Data
Names: Moore, Dinty W., 1955– author.
Title: The mindful writer / Dinty W. Moore.
Description: Somerville, MA : Wisdom Publications, 2016. | Includes index.
Identifiers: LCCN 2015041316| ISBN 9781614293521 (paperback) | ISBN
    161429352X (paperback)
Subjects: LCSH: Authorship—Miscellanea. | Authorship—Quotations, maxims,
    etc. | Authorship—Religious aspects—Buddhism. | BISAC: REFERENCE /
    Writing Skills. | LANGUAGE ARTS & DISCIPLINES / Composition &
    Creative Writing. | SELF-HELP / Creativity.
Classification: LCC PN165 .M66 2016 | DDC 808/.02—dc23
LC record available at http://lccn.loc.gov/2015041316

ISBN 978-1-61429-352-1   ebook ISBN 978-1-61429-370-5

20 19 18 17 16   5 4 3 2 1

Cover design by Phil Pascuzzo. Illustrations by Phil Pascuzzo. Interior design
by Gopa&Ted2. Set in Village 9.8/16.

Wisdom Publications' books are printed on acid-free paper and meet the
guidelines for permanence and durability of the Production Guidelines for Book
Longevity of the Council on Library Resources.

❦ This book was produced with environmental mindfulness.
For more information, please visit wisdompubs.org/wisdom-environment.

Printed in the United States of America.

Please visit fscus.org.

Dedicated to all sentient beings—
especially those struggling with the
arduous but magnificent koan
of the written word

Table of Contents

Introduction

WHY MINDFULNESS?

There are shelves full of books aiming to help beginning writers with every aspect of the writing craft, from character to scene, from image to metaphor, from plot to point of view, and beyond. All these are important elements to study and master, and many of the books are quite useful, but at its center, writing is a less complicated endeavor than these many texts suggest. I believe there are two primary skills that a writer needs to hone, skills that supersede the others, skills that need to be practiced and perfected not just at the beginning but throughout one's career.

The first skill a writer needs to cultivate is an

understanding of the inner workings of the sentence, paragraph, and page, just as a mechanic or engineer might learn how every working part of an engine propels an automobile forward. How do nouns best do their job? How do verbs suggest imagery in a reader's mind? What is the most efficient way of providing readers with as much information as possible—setting, tone, character motivation, voice—in the smallest number of words, while still writing elegant prose or poetry?

The second skill a writer must develop—one that goes beyond the adroit use of language—is the art of seeing with fresh eyes, thinking with an open mind, searching the nooks and crannies of any subject to find what has not yet been explored, or what might be explored further to shed some original light and engage the reader.

This book is aimed at helping writers nurture this second talent—seeing with fresh eyes and open mind—through a process known as mindfulness.

Let me expand: Too often beginning writers find themselves drawn to the common, customary, and comfortable conclusion or realization, to what we all seem to know and agree on as a culture: a moral of the story, so to speak. And why not? We have been shown all of our lives—in film, on television, via countless cultural messages—that certain ways of experiencing a subject are valid, acceptable, and safe.

To give just one instance, it is of course sad when a loved one dies, whether a cherished grandparent, a friend, or a spouse. It is true that our first reaction to the news is often one of shock, perhaps followed by a sense that "it is not fair . . . this person should be here still."

But as valid as that reaction is, it comes as no surprise to a reader, and more importantly, it does little to deepen the reader's (or writer's) understanding of death, loss, and the loneliness that often follows.

"Writers spend all their time preoccupied with just the things that their fellow men and women spend their time trying to avoid thinking about," the novelist and memoirist Harry Crews reflected some years ago. "It takes great courage to look where you have to look, which is in yourself, in your experience, in your relationship with fellow beings, your relationship to the earth, to the spirit or to the first cause—to look at them and make something of them."

That's the writer's job in a nutshell, to look "where you have to look." Or as the brilliant poet Mary Oliver puts it, "To pay attention, this is our endless and proper work."

You will see that this book speaks primarily to writers and often uses quotations from writers to make its key points.

The truth, however, is that the practice of seeing sharply and authentically, feeling what is honestly there to be felt, opening ourselves to emotions and experiences we might otherwise avoid, is part of every art form. Actors, painters, dancers, and musical composers have their own concerns and terminology, but they know very well that exploration and discovery are necessary to make art.

A final advantage of deliberate mindfulness is that it can help you to concentrate on your work—a true challenge in our modern, digital, gadget-driven world. Being mindful of what distracts you, of what leads you to walk away from your writing desk, of the inner voice that chides "don't bother, the work isn't good enough," is the first step to turning off those distractions, or voices, and getting the work done.

It isn't easy, but no one said it would be. Work is work, whether digging a ditch or, like the poet Seamus Heaney, digging in with your pen.

One last word, before we go forward. The practice of mindfulness is based in Eastern spiritual tradition, and much of my approach draws from the Buddhist tradition. But this book is ultimately about writing not religion, and you can be of any faith, or undecided, and still practice mindfulness.

Call it what you will, but by all means, slow down, listen, observe, and try to write the deeper truths.

THE FOUR NOBLE TRUTHS OF THE WRITING LIFE

As the author of *The Accidental Buddhist*, a memoir exploring my potholed attempts to fit Buddhist practice and philosophy into a typically busy, overindulgent modern lifestyle, I am often asked to explain how the Dharma teachings have influenced my writing. Despite the frequency of the question, however, for many years I found myself unable to provide anything close to a satisfying answer.

I knew that the Buddha's core teachings had seeped deep into my life, in ways that I had not originally anticipated, but I could not honestly say that my writing habits had changed as a result, or that I had taken on a "Buddhist approach" to the highly deliberate routine of choosing words, composing sentences, and accumulating pages. My work, it seemed, went on as it always had: ploddingly, unevenly, and with consistent difficulty.

Yet the question—"You are a Buddhist, so can you tell us how your Buddhism affects your writing?"—kept returning, and I kept offering feeble and evasive responses. Then one day it occurred to me: my inability to articulate a satisfying reply might mean that I was, in fact, trying all along to answer the wrong question. It was not Buddhism that had influenced my writing, but quite the opposite. The river of influence, perhaps, ran in the other direction. Rather than seeing mindfulness and Buddhism as shaping my efforts on the page, what I've come to understand is that my lifelong pursuit of writing and creativity helped to open me to the path of Buddhism. The innumerable lessons learned in struggling with my writing over the years had made me aware (albeit in an inarticulate, subconscious way) of the simple wisdom of mindfulness and nonattachment presented in the Buddha's Four Noble Truths.

Life is full of discontent, the Buddha told us, and that discontent (sometimes translated as suffering) comes about due to our grasping at things, our craving and clinging—the desire to make permanent what will always be fleeting. There is, however, a way to make the inescapabilty of discontent less problematic in our lives. The Way, the Path, is through right action, right speech, right livelihood; through living a deliberate and intentional life in service to the good of all living beings.

As a writer, I had learned the power of releasing my control of a story, of letting the words, the characters, the images, the mysterious underpinnings of a piece of prose take me in unexpected directions. The less I grasped at and choked my writing, the more it seemed to expand into areas that surprised and pleased not just me but the reader as well. Even my "noncreative" writing—business memos, application letters, proposals, and reports—were strengthened by this realization.

From the other end, I had seen how my ego and desires would inevitably lead me toward writer's block and self-loathing, how worrying about critical responses or negative reactions would eventually dry up whatever creative flow I had managed to bring forth.

I had come too to understand the importance of examining my motives for writing, of rooting out insincerity. Dishonest motives, such as writing to "get back" at someone who wronged you or pretending to be more decent or devout on the page than you are in real life, are as dangerous to a writer as just about anything I can name.

These lessons had already been learned and relearned many times over in my writing life, so when I first encountered the Four Noble Truths, they seemed familiar and true to my experience.

None of this is easy, of course. The deeper practice of intentional living and mindfulness remains an ongoing effort to be aware and awake, but at least I am not wondering if it all can work. I have seen with my own eyes, observed it directly, in my daily task.

How Does Mindfulness Work?

Practicing mindfulness teaches us to slow down, to listen, to hear what is actually there to be heard rather than what we expect to hear, and to then slow down even more and listen more deeply.

We listen to the world certainly: the birds outside our window, or the distant rumble of highway traffic. But we also listen to, and observe closely, those around us, seeing what they are doing, or saying, or not saying, or what they are indicating with their eyes and bodies, rather than merely seeing or hearing what's on the surface.

How many times have you had this conversation?

"Hey, how are you doing today?"

"Just great."

If we took those words at face value, we would assume the second person to speak is in fact feeling *just great*, but as we all know, that may or may not be the case. Part of mindfulness is hearing what is behind the words, perhaps something in the sound of the voice, or an expression on your friend's face, her body language, a certain hesitation or pause.

Finally, mindfulness teaches us to listen to ourselves, to the thoughts that pop up in our minds, even the thoughts that make us sad or uncomfortable. Perhaps especially those thoughts.

We also listen to, and watch, our reactions to those thoughts. Because it is here we will find the difficult questions, the unanswered concerns, the conundrums of what it is to be human in this complicated world.

Because that's where we need to go in our writing. That's the part where we might illuminate the darkness.

The Buddhist teacher Thich Nhat Hanh has written and lectured often on the subject of mindfulness, and he remains one of my most valued teachers because his message is so beautifully simple: if you want to promote peace, be peaceful as you walk across the room; if you want to promote love, love yourself and those immediately around you; if you want to reach enlightenment, be entirely awake and in the moment, whether awash in an oceanfront sunrise or merely washing the dinner dishes. Mindfulness begins with an awareness of the simplest action: breathing in, know that you are breathing in; breathing out, know that you are breathing out.

This may sound ridiculously basic, but this attentiveness is difficult—and it forms the heart of meditation. Through the simple awareness of breathing, you can eventually expand your mindfulness to the more complex and involuntary actions of your life.

For instance, when you are listening to your child, just home from school and crushed by the unkind teasing of a classmate, true mindfulness means that you are aware and present, hearing closely what your child is saying (not rushing to quickly dismiss the hurt feelings, or worrying that the problem is going to be a disruption in your busy day). Moreover, you remain alert, focused, listening—not distracted by the ringing telephone, the need for dinner preparation, or your own frustrations at the office.

In the context of writing, mindfulness means that at those moments when you are focusing on an elusive line of poetry or a stubborn plot obstacle in a story, you are able to remain attentive to the task at hand, seeing the words that are before you, hearing the possibilities in your mind, not succumbing to the thousands of other willing and ready distractions.

More than that, mindfulness means being aware of why you want to write, who you are writing for, and how to balance your desires for recognition with the demands of clear-headedness and honesty.

Finally, mindfulness includes a conscientious and thorough consideration of who you are as a writer, where you are in your life, what you are feeling, and what is inside of you that wants (or needs) to be written.

Or to put it another way, consider the Four Noble Truths, transposed into a writer's credo:

The Four Noble Truths for Writers

- The writing life is difficult, full of disappointment and dissatisfaction.

- Much of this dissatisfaction comes from the ego, from our insistence on controlling both the process of writing and how the world reacts to what we have written.

- There is a way to lessen the disappointment and dissatisfaction and to live a more fruitful writing life.

- The way to accomplish this is to make both the practice of writing and the work itself less about ourselves. To thrive, we must be mindful of our motives and our attachment to desired outcomes.

This book offers a series of quotations and brief responses to those quotations, illuminating how, in my view, writing and mindfulness can intersect in positive and productive ways.

The book is divided into four sections:

- **The Writer's Mind**: Where do writing and creativity originate?

- **The Writer's Desk**: What does mindfulness mean when you are directly at the task of writing?

- **The Writer's Vision**: How do writers mindfully engage their own writing, writing habits, and need for growth?

- **The Writer's Life**: What does it mean to be a writer in the world, to have dedicated oneself to the craft of writing?

You will find at the end of this book a few brief prompts aimed at helping us as writers to "see with fresh eyes," "hear with open ears," and "catch ourselves thinking." You need not wait until the end to try them, and you need not try them just once. They are meant to be attempted at any time, in any order, and kept near the writing desk, to be attempted again when your writing life needs a push forward.

One more note: in researching this book, I ran across quotes from equally experienced and accomplished authors that appeared to be in total contradiction. In trying to reconcile the divergent perspectives, I inevitably decided both views were correct. Accordingly, in all cases, the advice offered should be taken in the spirit of suggestion, not edict.

And remember this as well: just as we should avoid unproductive attachment to our own thoughts or words, it is not a good idea to cling too fiercely to the advice of others . . .

1

The Writer's Mind

1.

A writer is someone for whom writing is more difficult than it is for other people.

~ THOMAS MANN

BEING A WRITER can seem like a struggle at times: there is the challenge of trying to constantly refine the words that make up the stories you want to tell, and there is the difficulty of sustaining a belief in yourself and in the idea that your stories (or poems, or essays, or ideas) are of enough value that all of the work is worth the effort.

Yes, it can seem daunting, but Mann is assuring us that this is natural and fine. He is reminding us that iron is forged in fire, and the very fact that writing takes great determination—no matter who you are—is what makes the practice worth your effort.

So why is writing *more* difficult for the writer than for others?

Because we care about finding the precise word, the clearest expression, and we understand that sometimes a thought needs to be revised tens or hundreds of times before we find the perfect way to say what we really mean.

The good news? On the days it all seems too hard or nearly impossible, you can just reach around and pat yourself on the back.

The frustration simply means that you are going about it in the right way.

2.

The advice I like to give young artists, or really anybody who'll listen to me, is not to wait around for inspiration. Inspiration is for amateurs; the rest of us just show up and get to work.

~ CHUCK CLOSE

LET'S DISPENSE with inspiration from the start, because nothing causes more dissatisfaction and disappointment in a writer's life than the myth of the thunderbolt.

I have met, through the years, so many frustrated writers who have spent hour upon hour waiting for inspiration to arrive, waiting for that One Big Idea to land in their frontal lobes and fulfill their fantasies of becoming geniuses. Oh, I know the feeling well enough. I am not immune to the vagaries of desire. But artist after artist, writer after writer, will tell you that this is simply not how it works—and I know from my own experience that they speak the truth.

Instead of the lightning bolt to the forehead, the million-dollar insight, a writer finds the best ideas in trial and error, in sentences that start out one way and surprisingly, uncontrollably, end up pulling in another direction, in the toppled mess of a third draft that tumbles into a pile of half-finished thoughts.

This is perhaps the first and most important application of mindfulness for a writer:

Show up and get to work, as Close suggests, and at the same time, listen to where the writing wants to take you. Understand that the writing itself will often provide far richer material than your logical, predictable mind. Even more "intellect-driven" writing—for instance, a dissertation—can benefit from the cognitive leaps that occur when you stand back from the manuscript a moment and listen to your intuition.

Often our ideas about where we think a poem, story, or essay should go are all too willing to drown out the small whisper that is suggesting,

"No, that's not really as honest as this impulse over here. No, that's not quite right."

Listen to that whisper.

3.

Don't try to figure out what other people want to hear from you; figure out what you have to say. It's the one and only thing you have to offer.

~ BARBARA KINGSOLVER

NEARLY EVERY WRITER worries about having enough "material" to fill the page, or the chapter, or the book. We worry whether what we have written is worthy of attention, or whether we have exhausted all that we had to write about in the first place.

Writers worry as well about audience: Is what I am writing now what was popular last year? Is this the kind of writing that will be in vogue next year? Will I get the desired response from the reader, editor, agent with this sort of work?

And yet—to my mind—all of these worries are missing the point.

What we have is ourselves, and that is all we can really write about.

Now this is not to say you cannot enrich your experience. Your path as a writer may include travel to some foreign destination to chronicle the extreme hardships of poverty there. Or maybe you need to visit a neighborhood grocery store in a part of town to which you rarely venture, just to remind yourself of how rich a culture exists within your own city. Perhaps all you need to do is stop to talk for three minutes with the elderly neighbor up the street with whom you'd barely found the time to speak before. "So, how is your garden this year?"

Every writer does well to step away from the desk at regular intervals, to confront life where it is most tangible, most urgent: not on the page, but out in the world.

But even in these cases, only you can write about what *you* see, what *you* hear, what strikes *you* as important and significant. We have ourselves, our feelings, our reactions to the world, our insights, and the metaphors that spring to our minds. That is the clay with which we make our sculptures, the notes available to play our music.

But what if you are not interesting enough, you ask?

You are.

Yes, it may take some work on your part—to understand yourself, to explore those parts of your life and your mind that rest below the surface memory and thought. But the material *does surely* exist. The material always exists.

Notice how Kingsolver closes her quote: "It's the one and only thing you have to offer."

Make an honest offering, and readers will respond.

4.

There are significant moments in everyone's day that can make literature. That's what you ought to write about.

~ RAYMOND CARVER

CARVER'S ADVICE is the perfect companion to Kingsolver's recommendation.

If you are familiar with Carver's brilliant short stories, you know that they often focus on the simplest of daily interactions between people, on quiet exchanges, mundane events. His stories are told in simple language as well, in what came to be known as the "minimalist" style. And they are uniquely powerful, honest; they will invariably grab you in the gut. Because they are real.

Every life contains these moments, but not every writer knows to include them, not every writer sees them for what they are.

So how do you discover the significant moments in your own everyday life?

You sit. You listen.

5.

**When one is highly alert to language,
then nearly everything begs to be a poem.**

~JAMES TATE

TATE'S SUGGESTION invariably reminds me of
kinhin, or Zen-style walking meditation.

To be entirely honest, when I first began my
exploration of Buddhist practice, I never found
much value in the walking mediation sessions
that I experienced inside a crowded *zendo*, the
meditation hall. I understood that standing up
from the cushion and walking around the huge
room was partially intended to relieve stress in
the legs, to keep my feet from falling hopelessly
asleep, but the *kinhin* always came too late for me,
and instead of walking mindfully, I would end
up stumbling around on tingly, uncertain limbs,
focused entirely on not toppling into the person
directly in front of me. There seemed nothing
mindful, meditative, or useful about it.

But one warm June day, a Buddhist monastic from the Soto Zen tradition suggested we take our walking meditation outside, and for the next thirty minutes, she led us along trails and grassy hills, past a weathered barn and some deep-maroon hollyhocks, and, as the old saying goes, "over hill and dale." Like the flower petals themselves, the power of mindful walking opened clearly inside of me that day.

Later, back in the hushed meditation chamber, I was focused as never before, but not on the usual silence. Instead, I heard the insistent bird calls outside the window as if they were an unfamiliar language, as if I had suddenly landed on a distant planet full of delightful new aural sensations. But of course, it was the same planet—the one that I had been ignoring for thirty years.

Tate tells us that an awareness of language helps us to see the poem in all things, but I would add that an awareness of all things—not just lush farmland in the early summer, but crowded city streets, jarring suburban shopping centers, even those most unpleasant places, like airports—will open us up as writers, and help us to see the story or poem or play or monologue or memoir in everyone and everything.

6.

Compassion is a verb.

∼ THICH NHAT HANH

THE VIETNAMESE MONK Thich Nhat Hanh is not talking about writing here, or about grammar. He is reminding us to lift our compassionate selves off the cushion, to step away from our daily meditation spot and attend to the soup kitchen, the hospice, and other needs of the world around us.

But his reminder can be taken as writing advice as well.

Compassion is indispensable for an author. The fiction writer or playwright, for instance, must struggle to inhabit her characters, to understand who they are, what they need, what they want, and the obstacles that often stymie our characters' lives. The journalist must endeavor to discern the honest patterns in human behavior and the possible reasons for a given action. The memoirist faces a task similar to that of the novelist, though in this case the "characters" are actual people—family members, for instance. It takes consummate compassion to inhabit the truth of our families, especially if that truth is a troubled one.

Compassion has no room for blame, no need of right vs. wrong. Compassion requires that we understand—even if we disagree.

Here is a truism I regularly share with my writing students:

"No one wakes up in the morning and thinks, 'Today I am going to make an absolute mess of my life.' Yet this is what happens, time and again, to the people we know, to the people we hear about on the morning news shows, and to the people who populate our stories."

It is our job, as writers, to imagine why human beings, often even those with the best intentions, seem consistently to create disarray, both ·personal and public. It is our job as well to understand that these failings could happen to anyone.

Exercise the muscles that compassionately open the heart.

In your writing and your life.

7.

**There is a vitality, a life force, an energy . . .
that is translated through you into action,
and because there is only one of you in all
of time, this expression is unique. And if
you block it, it will never exist through any
other medium and it will be lost.
The world will not have it.**

~ MARTHA GRAHAM

GRAHAM IS SPEAKING here of the necessity of honoring your individuality, your specificity, the essence of who you are. Don't fear your eccentricity or oddness, she counsels. Embrace it.

Moreover, it is only by being attentive to your own vitality and distinct energy, examining and understanding the underpinnings of your thoughts and actions—another sort of mindfulness—that you will be able to bring your perspective forward. Without this attention, the poems you were meant to write will never be written.

Graham composed in a different medium. She

was a modern dance choreographer, a pioneer of a new art form. Instead of words on the page, she used movement and the human body to craft her message. Still, her doubts about her own work, her painful insecurity, would be familiar to any writer.

Listen to what she had to say about *those* moments:

> It is not your business to determine how good it is nor how valuable nor how it compares with other expressions.
>
> It is your business to keep it yours clearly and directly, to keep the channel open.

8.

Find out the reason that commands you to write; see whether it has spread its roots into the very depth of your heart; confess to yourself you would have to die if you were forbidden to write.

~RAINER MARIA RILKE

WRITING IS HARD, yes. There are days, in fact, when it will seem too difficult to continue, when language and words and ideas will seem to have formed into a sort of cement just moments away from becoming solid, impenetrable. There is no way you can work with that inflexible substance.

And yet you do.

Because you have to.

Not because you want to write, but because you *must*.

To my mind, Rilke is acknowledging the joy of writing here as well. Despite the day-to-day frustrations any artist faces, there is nothing more thrilling, more exhilarating, than knowing that what you are doing matters, that it is important, that it is what you were meant to be doing.

This feeling is what sustains us, what makes us so fortunate to have woken up one morning and thought to ourselves, "I want to make something new."

9.

What crazies we writers are, our heads full of language like buckets of minnows standing in the moonlight on a dock.

~HAYDEN CARRUTH

I USED TO FISH along the shoreline of Lake Erie as a boy and still have a firm visual memory of minnows, in a bucket, reflecting the afternoon light.

Carruth's metaphor, I think, is perfect. If you have ever tried to catch a minnow in a net, or your hand, as it darts left, right, forward, and sometimes—it seems—backward, you understand very well what he is saying. The exact thought, the precise phrase or adjective, can be just as elusive as that minnow, just as frustrating to catch.

How many times have you thought or said, *"If I could only think of the right word . . ."*? It is not only poets who struggle with the elusiveness of language. It applies to all writing, even the memo you write to other office workers at your day job.

And there is more: Catching that minnow is not just difficult, it is *deceptively* difficult. When you are looking down into the bucket, the minnow is small, the net is so big, and that little fish has no place to hide. It should be easy.

We often imagine that writing will be easy in this way too. After all, we know what we want to say—all we have to do is say it.

But it turns out we *are* crazy. What are minnows but brief flashes? And what are thoughts?

And how do you capture a brief flash, even for a second?

10.

The depth is in the surface.

~WILLIAM MATTHEWS

PERMIT ME to quote Thich Nhat Hanh again:

"If you are a poet," he writes, "you will see clearly that there is a cloud floating in (every) sheet of paper. Without a cloud, there will be no rain; without rain, the trees cannot grow; and without trees, we cannot make paper. The cloud is essential for the paper to exist."

Some folks will look at a blank piece of paper and see nothing but a white field of emptiness. Others, the more mindful, will see what is really there: clouds, rain, trees, sunshine. They understand how none of these things can exist without the other.

Or put another way, being mindful of the origins of things—paper for instance—creates connections. Underneath every surface, below every common thought, behind each and every cliché, there is depth, if you will only take the time to look.

It is easy enough to see the surface of things, yet in truth, there are times we can't even accomplish that much. Often, instead of seeing what is there, all we see is what we anticipate will be there, our own attachments and expectations.

The mindful writer strives to see the true surface, and then to see the depth as well.

11.

**Confront the dark parts of yourself.
Your willingness to wrestle with your
demons will cause your angels to sing.**

~ AUGUST WILSON

MANY WRITERS, whether playwrights like Wilson, or poets, or essayists, or fiction writers, have said much the same thing: focus your writing on what makes you uncomfortable, explore the material that you'd really rather not explore.

Why?

Well, the subject matter—whatever it is—bothers you for a reason. The urge to turn aside does not come from nowhere. There is energy in your discomfort. Urgency and power. Call it what you will—reverse magnetic pull?

So it is simple enough:

If your goal is to have energy, urgency, power in your words, then do not ignore these impulses.

Embrace them.

12.

For me, writing starts with a line, or some imagination, or some notion, and I just go with it as far as I can. And you know how this works, this idea that you sort of set yourself afloat on the language.
And you think, I'll see how far it can take me before this little raft I've cobbled together falls apart and everybody understands that I'm really just a fraud, or drowning—whichever comes first.

~ THOMAS LYNCH

THE LITTLE RAFT is a wonderful description of what happens when the writing is working, when the ideas are afloat and the language is a river moving you gently forward.

If you have ever floated along on a raft or kayak, you know just what a wonderful feeling it is when the water takes you downstream at a comfortable but insistent pace. You'd be happy enough to float there forever, feeling the current, the effortless flow.

One of my favorite books of all time is Eugen Herrigel's *Zen in the Art of Archery*. The idea at the center of the book seems a riddle: you can only hit the target by not aiming at the target. You can only achieve your objective when you cease clinging to and grasping at the outcome you desire.

Lynch's quote here nicely echoes Herrigel's Zen lesson. Writing fails most often when the writer fights against the flow of the writing, when the writer refuses to set himself "afloat on the language," when the writer grasps too firmly or aims too hard.

Lynch, of course, knows that no river current flows smoothly forever; inevitably you will hit a snag—maybe a dead tree limb crossing from bank to bank. For Lynch, that dead limb is his fear and insecurity. He is a fraud, he fears, or he has lost his way.

The quote goes on a bit further, with Lynch reminding us that when we *do* set ourselves afloat, "when it's really working, the reader goes with you to the most unlikely places."

13.

Even in literature and art, no man who bothers about originality will ever be original: whereas if you simply try to tell the truth (without caring twopence how often it has been told before) you will, nine times out of ten, become original without ever having noticed it. Give up yourself, and you will find your real self.

~C. S. LEWIS

LEWIS SOUNDS remarkably like a Zen teacher, perhaps one attempting to explain the most notoriously bewildering of Buddhist concepts, the notion of "no self," or like a Zen master urging his student to discover the Original Self.

What I understand Lewis to be saying, however, is that there are no "original" thoughts or ideas, as in "look how clever I am, because I came up with this before anyone else."

There is simply the truth of our being, who we are as human beings on this odd planet, how we live our lives, and a writer captures that truth not through cleverness and guile, but by listening, observing, recording.

14.

In the stories we tell ourselves,
we tell ourselves.

~ MICHAEL MARTONE

HERE IS A CONVERSATION I've had countless times, in my own head:

> *So what am I going to write about?*
> *I could write about myself.*
> *But that's not interesting.*
> *But that's what I know about best of all.*
> *Well, how uninteresting of you.*
> *So what do I write about?*
> **Sigh**

Does that sound at all familiar?

Maybe your inner voices are not quite so animated, but nonetheless, common writer's insecurity will insure that you have experienced some version of this concern not once but most likely repeatedly, throughout your writing life.

Martone knows that the answer to this riddle

is simple enough—we have no alternative. Even when writing about distant lands, or events far in the past, or people and places greatly removed, we are still telling the same story—the story we tell ourselves, which is the story of who we are.

Why do I like this quote so much? It gives me the freedom to set my worry aside.

I'm writing too much about myself.

Well, I have no choice.

So what are the stories I tell myself? How can I capture them? And what do they mean? Not on the surface, but truly, honestly, in depth?

Now *that's* interesting enough to sustain a lifetime of writing.

15.

It is necessary to write, if the days are not to slip emptily by. How else, indeed, to clap the net over the butterfly of the moment? For the moment passes, it is forgotten; the mood is gone; life itself is gone. That is where the writer scores over his fellows: he catches the changes of his mind on the hop.

~ VITA SACKVILLE-WEST

WHY DO WE WRITE? Yes, there are days that the answer might be as shallow as "I want to see my name in the table of contents of *The Paris Review*" or "I want to be one of those smart people interviewed in a magazine and then show that magazine to my older sisters who always implied that I was too dim-witted to accomplish anything."

But those reasons will not sustain a writer, certainly not through the inevitable rejection, the agonizing dry spells, the stinging eyeballs and tired brain cells that come halfway through a book project.

We write to capture a bit of ourselves and a bit of the world that is floating (and occasionally hurtling at incredible speed) past the window of our lives. We write to clap the net over the butterfly that is our very existence.

Letting "the days slip emptily by" is as close to a definition of the opposite of mindfulness as I can imagine. Be the one who catches "the changes of his mind on the hop," by making writing a necessity, a fortunate itch that must be scratched.

After all, what is the use of being alive if you don't stop every once in a while and marvel at the very wonder of it?

16.

**To me the greatest pleasure of writing is
not what it's about, but the music
the words make.**

~ TRUMAN CAPOTE

AND THAT IS the other reason we write.

Because what results from our efforts is irresistible to us.

"Do you think I can be a writer?" students will sometimes ask me. They think they are asking about innate talent, or raw intelligence, or whether they exhibit a sufficient amount of noteworthy thought and insight.

My answer is much simpler than that, however.

"I don't know," I say to them. "Do you love playing with words?"

It is the very texture of language, the primal clay of verbs, nouns, sentences, the tactile sensation of combining those words into a poem or story, that in the end will bring a writer her most satisfaction.

Glory and recognition are fleeting—but loving what you do, in the moment that you are doing it, is an incomparable gift.

17.

Your poem effectively begins at the first moment you've surprised or startled yourself.

~STEPHEN DUNN

THIS IS IT EXACTLY, what you are looking for. It may take ten lines, or twenty sentences, or fifty pages until you reach that moment, but the moment will come if you are open to it, if you pay attention to the movement of the mind.

Stay awake! Be startled.

And don't despair the false starts: just scratch them out and move forward.

2

The Writer's Desk

18.

**The more I write, the more I think that
everything you've done up to the point
that you're writing isn't much help.
You always start out in the dark.**

~ CHARLES BAXTER

MANY YEARS AGO, in one of my first writing classes, I asked the seasoned novelist at the head of the table, "Vance, does it get easier to write a book after you've written and published so many?"

He smiled, opening his hands in a sort of shrug-like gesture.

"No," he said. "It just gets harder each time, because with each book you write, you become more and more aware of the possibilities, of where a story can go. So with each scene, each sentence, you have so many more options, so many more choices to cycle through."

Vance thought a moment, and then added: "Plus, every time you start a new book, you give yourself a challenge, and if you are a real writer, you make sure that challenge is even more impossible than the challenge you faced in the previous work."

The students in the room that day groaned with disappointment. We wanted the writing to get easier. We wanted our teacher to say, "Yes, it actually becomes a piece of cake."

Now my own students occasionally ask the same question of me, and the answer (Sorry, kids!) is always "No! It doesn't seem to get any easier at all."

Now, to be completely honest, that's not *entirely* true. Some aspects of writing become a bit easier—for instance, with practice you become better at knowing when to strike out a sentence, knowing when to dump an entire page and just start from scratch. You've made so many mistakes that a few of them become easy to spot.

But still, you are always starting out in the dark, striking out for new territory.

Now here's the good news:

This starting out in the dark, having to discover all over again what makes words work on
the page, is what keeps it exciting, interesting,
maddening—and so worth the effort.

Mindfulness in one's own life works much
the same way: you discover new aspects of who
you are, you see the world in fresh ways, your
understanding of what is possible is constantly
renewed.

Mindfulness, for all of its simplicity, is a powerful practice.

19.

The writer operates at a peculiar crossroads where time and place and eternity somehow meet.
His problem is to find that location.

~FLANNERY O'CONNOR

WE KNOW from her writings that O'Connor was deeply spiritual, identifying strongly with the Catholic tradition. Still, in my view, she is talking here about enlightenment.

The Sanskrit word for enlightenment, *bodhi*, means "awakened." My early forays into Buddhism included all of the common misconceptions, including the persistent idea that enlightenment is the final goal and that once enlightenment was attained, the ethereal Buddhist would sit blissfully atop a mountain, perhaps glowing and smiling at the lesser beings trudging along the path below.

That, of course, is utter nonsense. Enlightenment is of no use unless it is employed to better the world for all beings, and enlightenment—like any awakening—can come and go. Indeed, it can be very fleeting.

Writers who struggle with a poem, or story, or essay, for draft after draft after draft, may on occasion experience a smidgen of enlightenment. It is the moment that the perfect word, or precise action by a character, or the ideal phrasing of an idea is revealed to the writer.

So often, this ideal phrase or line of dialogue is more of a discovery than an invention. It is a flash, like the proverbial light bulb above the head depicted in cartoons. This flash of insight doesn't come from thinking, from intellect, or from reason; it comes instead from a more mysterious part of our awareness. For that moment at least, it can seem as if time and place and eternity have somehow met.

For the writer, the problem is to find that "peculiar crossroads," the ever-shifting "location" where insight forms.

And then, once the story or poem is finished, it is time to start anew, and the search begins again.

20.

Catch yourself thinking.

~ ALLEN GINSBERG

BUDDHISTS HAVE a term—monkey mind—that portrays the restlessness of our brains, especially when we try to deliberately slow the brain down.

If you have ever attempted to meditate, you know how this works. The brain is likely to go suddenly hyperactive, leaping from notion to notion, idea to idea, like a caffeine-fueled monkey swinging from tree to tree. Just when you think the mind's stream of thought has slowed down, that you can stop and lay a finger on a single notion, the monkey goes flying off to another tree, and then another.

In meditation, the goal (eventually, after many years of gradual effort) is to find the truth that is beyond thought. A useful exercise along the way, however, is to on occasion just forget the "no thought" idea—which can be distracting itself—and instead intentionally focus on the chatter of the mind. Just watch and listen as it runs its course.

It can be a fascinating exercise to take whatever insistent thought that pops up—be it serious or trivial—and let it swing on and on to as many trees and branches as it desires, until it—the distraction itself—is seemingly exhausted, run to the ground, out of steam.

Ginsberg doesn't advise us to stop the monkey from his inevitable traveling, just to catch the moment, to pull out a single thought for an instant and really notice, be mindfully aware.

That thought is a line of a poem, the beginning of a story, an essay.

Catch it.

21.

**When I face the desolate impossibility of writing five hundred pages, a sick sense of failure falls on me and I know I can never do it. This happens every time.
Then gradually I write one page and then another.**

~ JOHN STEINBECK

THAT SICK SENSE of failure is inevitable, I'm afraid. I've never met a writer who didn't struggle with it occasionally—or often.

But you alone can control whether or not this sick feeling of dread defeats you.

If you let it drive you away from the keyboard or compel you to put down the pen, you have been defeated, and the forces of failure have won.

What to do instead?

Sit with it.

Know that it is normal.

Wait for it to pass—as all things do.

22.

A writer is a writer not because she writes well and easily, because she has amazing talent, because everything she does is golden. In my view, a writer is a writer because even when there is no hope, even when nothing you do shows any sign of promise, you keep writing anyway.

~JUNOT DÍAZ

DÍAZ IS ECHOING Steinbeck here: a book or story is completed by writing one page after another, by enduring the doubt and discomfort and remaining on the job.

This ability, to keep on despite no "sign of promise," can be nurtured and strengthened.

How? By being mindful of the drought times, the patches where your writing is slow or non-existent. What causes them? What voices arise in your head to discourage you? What does it feel like to want to write and yet come up wordless, without voice?

Be mindful as well of what eventually snaps the dry streak. How does it end? How does it feel when it ends?

And most importantly, take note that it *does* end.

Memorize that moment and the feeling of release that comes when you start writing again. Use that memory as a salve, a tool, a prompt.

Or at the very least, as a reminder: a refuge.

Nothing—not even writer's block!—lasts forever.

23.

**Writing a novel is like driving a car
at night. You can see only as far as your
headlights, but you can make
the whole trip that way.**

~ E. L. DOCTOROW

THE CHINESE PHILOSOPHER Lao Tzu is often remembered for his observation, "The longest journey begins with a single step."

Well, each and every writing project begins with the writing of one word.

That's not so hard, is it?

That one word might eventually be crossed out, in fact, so what you put down doesn't even have to be the *right* word, or even a good one. Just a word.

Put one word in front of the other and, soon enough, you have a sentence, a paragraph, a page.

A page!

A page may not seem like much, but the pages add up fast. How many pages does it take to write a book? If you write five pages per week, how many weeks will it take to reach your goal?

Time can be the enemy, but time can also be a friend.

Don't dwell on how far that road ahead might be. Just think as far as your headlights can reach, and keep on driving.

One day you will look up and see that you have reached your destination.

And there begin your next journey.

24.

If you don't feel that you are possibly on the edge of humiliating yourself, of losing control of the whole thing, then probably what you are doing isn't very vital.
If you don't feel like you are writing somewhat over your head, why do it?
If you don't have some doubt of your authority to tell this story, then you are not trying to tell enough.

~ JOHN IRVING

THE TRUE WORK of the writer is the true work of all artists: to take risks, to lean far out over the edge of the accepted truth, to see what can only be seen from that vantage point.

Ask yourself every once in a while: Am I in over my head? Am I posing questions in my work to which there can never be satisfying, final answers? Am I trying to tackle a project here that is well beyond my capacity as a writer? Am I just a little afraid of the direction that all of this is going?

If the answer to each of these questions is yes, then you are heading in the right direction.

Steady on.

25.

Every morning between 9 and 12, I go to my room and sit before a piece of paper. Many times, I just sit for three hours with no ideas coming to me. But I know one thing: If an idea does come between 9 and 12, I am there ready for it.

~ FLANNERY O'CONNOR

BUDDHISTS—especially Zen Buddhists—who have devoted themselves to life in a monastery will often meditate for most of the waking day. Some of this might be a form of what is called "working meditation": the mindful chopping of vegetables for the monastery supper, the mindful sweeping of the monastery courtyard, the washing of the monastery's laundry. But much of the day, the majority often, is spent simply sitting, on a cushion, in silence.

To outsiders, what happens on the cushion often seems a great mystery, and all sorts of myths have arisen about what really happens in the meditation hall. I, for one, have never seen anyone levitate, and I'm pretty sure no one has ever been struck by a golden thunderbolt while I was in the room.

At my first meditation retreat, a challenging five days of long silent sessions, to just about every question I asked during our nightly interview the teacher would smile mysteriously and answer, "Just sit."

Yes, part of the reason for meditation is that the monks are in some sense seeking enlightenment, the clear mind of the Buddha, the falling away of misconception and attachment. But mainly they are just sitting, being there, attempting to remain open and receptive to all that arises.

You can't plan for enlightenment. It doesn't arrive like frequent flyer rewards. You don't log a certain number of hours on the *zafu* in order to be guaranteed the journey. Enlightenment comes when it comes, and no one can ever know when that might be.

So the monks will sit. And sit. And they will study scripture, speak with senior teachers, chant a bit, perhaps. And then they will sit some more.

On those days that nothing good seems to come from sitting on the cushion, in front of your keyboard, maybe you can imagine that you are the Zen monk, waiting.

The words will come eventually.

You just never know when.

26.

Convince yourself that you are working in clay, not marble; on paper, not eternal bronze: let that first sentence be as stupid as it wishes.

~ JACQUES BARZUN

ONE SECRET that so many accomplished writers know and many beginning writers have yet to discover is the freedom and importance of lousy first drafts.

Writing, after all, is an illusion of sorts. When I pick up a novel written by a gifted writer, it seems that every word is precisely where it needs to be, every metaphor is apt and vivid, and every movement of plot or idea is natural and inevitable. The story is so good, I hear myself thinking, that it couldn't have been written any other way.

It is a short leap from such thoughts to imagining that the writer is a genius of some sort, gifted in ways that mere mortals will never be gifted.

That writer in your imagination sits down at the desk—usually this imaginary desk is highly polished, of rare wood, centered in an airy, immaculate room, facing a window with a view of the infinite sea—puts fingers to keyboard or pencil to pad and these perfect, breathtaking, inevitable words, images, scenes, and ideas simply flow onto the page.

I have had this fantasy, I know.

But I have also had occasion to talk with countless accomplished writers, and what they'll say again and again is, "You should have seen what a mess this was at the beginning." Or, "Believe me, for the first ten drafts I had no idea what this was even going to be about." Or, "Man, I sweated blood on this thing and thought it would never resolve itself."

Lousy first drafts allow you to have a base, something to which you can respond. Those lousy first drafts are not carved into marble; they are carved into soft clay, and they can be formed, and reformed, and reformed again, endlessly. As they should.

So give yourself permission to write that lousy first draft, or let that first sentence "be as stupid as it wishes."

Don't fall for the illusion.

Successful writing takes great exertion, and multiple revisions, refinement, retooling—until it looks as if it didn't take any effort at all.

27.

You can only have bliss
if you don't chase it.

~BHANTE GUNARATANA

WANTING TO BE a writer, wanting to be published, wanting to sell a boatload of books, wanting to be recognized with prizes, accolades, and reviews, no matter how desperately you want these things, will never take you where you want to go.

Wanting to write something true and important will take you there.

If you write it.

28.

**Don't tell me the moon is shining;
show me the glint of light on broken glass.**

~ ANTON CHEKHOV

MINDFULNESS, of course, is not limited to an awareness of your writing rituals and habits, or simply listening to the workings of your monkey mind. Mindfulness can extend to the sentences you put on the page. Are you painting the full picture?

It is never enough that *you* see the scene that exists in your mind. It is never enough that *you* can imagine the sunset on that driftwood-scattered beach. Nor is it ever enough that *you* see and feel the rough wool of the brown overcoat itching and scratching at your neck.

The reader needs to see and feel it as well.

One practical use for mindfulness—total concentration and openness to what is directly before you—is the way in which this practice allows you to read your own writing, with preconceptions and attachments set momentarily aside. With proper focus, you can engage your own words as if they were written by someone else, someone without your memory, experience, or intentions.

This practice works in poetry, fiction, and playwriting, but also when composing a memo at the office, or sending a letter of complaint or request. There is what you think you are saying, and then there is what the words on the page actually say.

Learn the difference.

Reveal the glint of light on broken glass.

29.

It seems to me that those songs that have been any good, I have nothing much to do with the writing of them. The words have just crawled down my sleeve and come out on the page.

~ JOAN BAEZ

BAEZ'S OBSERVATION might at first seem to be urging us away from mindfulness. Baez appears to be saying that her mind has little or nothing to do with her creativity; that the words in her songs come from somewhere else.

As a teacher, I am often instructing my students to let go of the tight grasp they have on their work, to release the iron-grip of control. The poem wants to go where the poem wants to go, not where you want to take it, I tell them. The characters have a better idea of where this story goes next than you probably do. You think this essay is about your sister's car accident but it really wants to be an essay about jealousy.

Scientists, too, sometimes share stories of how thinking "outside the box" led them to a revelation they would never have reached through logic and conventional thinking.

This advice is difficult for inexperienced writers to hear. Often as not, when I go down this road, the student will look at me as if I were spouting nonsense.

But I'm not. The longer I've been at this crazy business of catching minnows in a bucket, the more I invariably trust that eventually the work takes over, the story or poem or essay accumulates its own momentum. It becomes my job not to guide it so much as to follow where it leads.

To do so, however, you need to be focused, mindful enough to sense that faint voice, recognize that line of poetry, refrain of a song, or snippet of unexpected dialogue, crawling down your sleeve.

Don't be that writer who gets in the way, stifling the very words that want to be written.

30.

Writing teaches writing.

~ JOHN MCPHEE

"How do I become a better writer?"

"Just write."

"And then what?"

"Keep writing."

"And then eventually . . . ?"

"You write."

"Until?"

"Until you have written something."

"Then what?"

"You get up out of bed the next morning and write some more."

This is my version of a Zen koan.

31.

You have to sweep the temple steps a lot in hopes that the god appears.

~ DEAN YOUNG

THE ZEN TEACHER John Tarrant has suggested that enlightenment—or any form of spiritual awakening—is a sort of accident. He adds, however, the reminder that "the spiritual work of silence and stillness makes us accident-prone . . ."

Dean Young is saying much the same thing, I believe. To be sweeping the temple steps a long time can be taken as a simple metaphor for sticking with one's spiritual practice, whether it is daily meditation, regular prayer, mindfulness, or writing. It might be taken as yet another reminder to the writer to keep her energy focused on her task, to remain in that seat facing the tablet or keyboard, waiting for the exact right words to appear.

As writers, we want to remain accident-prone, ready for that cheerful calamity when an image or idea comes to us from seemingly nowhere, or two phrases we splice together once again show how the sum can be so much greater than the parts. Yes, writing is a deliberate act, and there is serious cognitive activity involved, but there is also magic, serendipity, what some call grace.

Be open to it, be ready for it, be present on the temple steps—and you too will find that for which you have been waiting.

32.

Love the writing, love the writing, love the writing . . . the rest will follow.

~JANE YOLEN

SOME ADVICE is simple enough. If you love what you do, the rest will follow.

But what if you don't? There are always those days, doubt-filled, anguished. Nothing wants to come out. Each word is a struggle, and even then the word doesn't suit. Your mind, it seems, has changed from powerful muscle to nebulous mist.

Well, that's why you need to love the writing like you love your children, your parents, your siblings, your spouse, or your dearest friend. Goodness knows, each of those relationships can be fraught with difficulty, but even if you need to take a break, even if faced with an extended period of disappointment or anger, if you truly love the person, you always come back.

You can't *not* come back.

That's one definition of love.
So love the writing.
The rest will sort itself out, in the end.

3

The Writer's Vision

33.

We do not write to be understood.
We write in order to understand.

~ C. DAY LEWIS

TO MY MIND, the worst writers in any medium fail because they have an idea and sit down with no better intention than to "explain" the brilliant idea to the readers.

It doesn't work that way. Writing is not explaining. Writing is not the mere description of an idea. To write requires learning, discovering, examining, and interrogating. Writing is the process of putting down words, then stepping back, considering those words, trying to understand them.

What have you written? What does it say? What does it fail to say? Do you even agree with what you have written?

That last question is crucial.

Just because something has been set down on

the page doesn't mean it is true, as tempting as it might be to think so. Even if you are the one who put the words onto the page—*especially* if you are the one who put the words onto the page— the words are not necessarily accurate. If you have been paying attention in your life, you have certainly seen instances where certain ideas and notions can *ring* true without actually *being* true.

There are countless companion quotes to this one from C. Day Lewis, wherein writers reveal that it is in the very act of writing and then revising what they have written that thoughts begin to coalesce, that partial theories begin to take shape and become whole, that the writer discovers and understands what needs to be said.

If you simply sit at your desk waiting for that wonderful idea, so you can transcribe it onto the page, or if you merely settle for first drafts, assuming "good enough" is good enough, you are missing out on what is so fascinating and absorbing about being a writer, and you will likely find yourself having written dead or predictable essays, poems, stories, or, yes, even business letters.

34.

Anyone who puts pen to paper can have a prose style. In almost every case, that style will be quiet, sometimes so quiet as to be detectable only by you, the writer.
In the quiet, you can listen to your sound in various manifestations; then you can start to shape it and develop it.
That project can last as long as you keep writing, and it never gets old.

~BEN YAGODA

MANY WRITERS struggle with voice or style, and for good reason. Finding a comfortable voice can be a daunting task.

Yet voice is what makes writing distinctive, what creates a Kurt Vonnegut, a Maxine Hong Kingston, a Dorothy Parker, or a Rita Dove.

When readers say they love a certain writer's work, it is quite often the voice and style they have fallen in love with.

So why is finding your authentic voice so hard?

One reason is that most of us were taught in school to sound exactly the same. We were trained toward a certain stiffness, a formality, and we were given so many rules to follow that the simplest response was to write the sentences that seemed familiar, safe, approved. Academic writing and most writing in the corporate or business world is expected to sound the same, no matter who wrote it. There is no room set aside for individual voice in a scientific study or budget summary.

But you are you, not everyone else, and that essence of you is important to the poem, the story, the memoir, the novel.

Writing is very much about listening:

First you listen to the world around you.

Then you listen to your own reactions to that world. Not the easy, cliché reactions, but the honest ones, the contradictory ones, the unexpected ones; the reactions that take some time to even recognize.

And then you listen to how you express those

reactions. Where is the "you" in what you have seen, said, and thought? Is that "you" so quiet that maybe only you can detect it?

Maybe it is, but as Yagoda suggests, part of your work is to shape and develop your voice—starting with that quiet whisper.

35.

The writing of a poem is like a child throwing stones into a mineshaft. You compose first, then you listen for the reverberation.

~JAMES FENTON

LIKE YAGODA'S ADVICE in the previous section, Fenton is stressing the importance of the ear. Listen to what you have written. Listen for meaning. Listen for sound. Listen for the unexpected reverberations.

By listening, of course, I don't mean sitting in silence and just "hearing the words" in your head. I heartily advise reading your words out loud, as you write them, after the first draft, and again after the tenth and twentieth draft.

Out loud.

So the cat can hear as well.

So that the neighbors worry you are talking to ghosts.

Even if at first the awkwardness of what you

have written makes you cringe—read your words aloud, and listen.

Listen closely.

Trust your ear.

36.

**The real voyage of discovery consists
not in seeing new landscapes
but in having new eyes.**

~ MARCEL PROUST

MINDFULNESS MEANS seeing the actual picture rather than the picture you expect to see.

Photographers will often speak of this. There are those who lift the camera's viewfinder to their eye and, for whatever reason, search for the conventional photograph: the boat in the sunset, the mountains at a distance, the tourist smiling in front of the shrine. Of course, there is nothing wrong with such photographs—they serve as a nice record of the vacation or moment—but they are not going to startle the viewer, or cause the viewer to reconsider her world.

It is exactly the same in writing. There are certain expected observations, anticipated reactions. Seeing with new eyes will get you beyond those.

Proust is also telling us that we needn't visit

a Thai jungle, a Paris café, or the horn of Africa to discover fresh territory and rich inspiration.

Take your new eyes out the front door of your house, and see all that is to be seen right there.

37.

**Write as if you were dying. At the same
time, assume you write for an audience
consisting solely of terminal patients.
That is, after all, the case.
What would you begin writing
if you knew you would die soon?
What could you say to a dying person that
would not enrage by its triviality?**
~ ANNIE DILLARD

YOU MIGHT EXPECT that when someone chooses
to meditate on a particular image or object, that
person would choose a flickering candle or a fresh
tangerine sitting out in the rain. Something lovely,
full of life and light.

Sometimes they do.

Monks from various Buddhist traditions,
however, as part of their training, are sent up
the mountainside to meditate beside a decaying
corpse. Yes, an actual corpse.

Why? To reinforce the concept of impermanence. No one lives forever. Nothing stays the same.

Human beings waste vast energies attempting to stave off the inevitable, trying to pretend that the world will never change, that what we build—cities, governments, fortunes, our relationships with others—can be made to stay exactly as they are, pristine and untouched by decay.

Humans sometimes seem to be in full denial mode, especially about the one truth, which is that we all die eventually. Everyone. No exceptions.

If we *really* acknowledged this fact, maybe we might not waste so much of our time here on the planet, consuming mindlessly, spinning on our own wheels, prolonging petty battles.

If you knew you were dying, to what project would you choose to devote your efforts, each and every day that you had left?

Well you *are* dying, Dillard is reminding you, not soon hopefully, but eventually.

So what *should* you be doing?

38.

The truth you believe in and cling to makes you unavailable to hear anything new.

~ PEMA CHÖDRÖN

A CRUCIAL ASPECT of mindfulness is becoming aware of what we cling to and recognizing the clichés in our own thinking or beliefs. There are notions that stick in our brains the way plaque adheres to the arteries of our heart, and neither of these is good for us.

If something has seemed to be true for as long as you can remember, it is easy to begin imagining that this belief is *unassailably* true, that it is incontrovertible, because it has always seemed so, because it has stood the test of time. But in fact, time is not much of a test. Ask Galileo, for instance.

The only true test is examination. Why do I believe that? Is it merely convenient to believe that? Is this belief comfortable because it lets me off the hook? Do I just believe this idea or truism because my mother, my father, my priest, my friend told it to me?

The mindful thinker is relentless, always challenging.

39.

The genuine writer relinquishes blame, struggles for understanding.

~VALERIE MINER

THIS IS SO IMPORTANT.

Let's say you are writing about your childhood, a nonfiction account perhaps, or a loosely fictionalized version. As you write and remember, there are multiple variations of you sitting in front of that word processing screen or tablet:

There is the wounded nine-year-old you, still (because childhood can be so searingly painful) aching after all of these years.

There is the angry teenage you, still needing somehow to rebel, to lash out.

There is the twenty-something you who finally recognized how much pain and anger there was in your childhood and that what seemed normal to the youngster was neither normal nor healthy.

And perhaps there is the forty-three- or sixty-three-year-old you, sitting at the desk, trying to explain and explore the memories that somehow never go away.

Whose perspective are you going to bring to the work?

That is not a simple question—there is no right or wrong answer, or one-size-fits-all. Any one of these particular points of view, from a specific vantage point in your life, might be exactly what is needed to allow the reader to discover the deeper currents of your life. But which one?

Be mindful that the teenager's point of view, the angry "it was your fault, it was your fault, it was your fault!!" perspective, runs the risk of hitting just one note, a note that may be a dead-end, both psychologically and as a narrative tool.

Likewise, the child's point of view, innocent and purely the victim, though sympathetic, can stifle the ability for exploration. There is often too much the child doesn't understand.

Of course, the adult point of view can be just as limiting, if the adult in question is still looking to place blame, to prove that the other people in the story were wrong.

There is no reason to tackle a subject, even your own life story, if you are not seeking understanding, looking to learn something, asking questions to which you do not know the answer.

That is what will make the work interesting to the reader, and that is what will make the process worthwhile for you.

40.

**I write to find out what I'm thinking,
what I'm looking at, what I see,
and what it means.**

~JOAN DIDION

**How do I know what I think
until I see what I say?**

~E. M. FORSTER

THERE ARE COUNTLESS QUOTES from countless writers expressing this very sentiment, but here I share just two of my favorites.

Writing is not the act of recording a fully formed insight; it is trial and error, a way to experiment with an idea. Our first thoughts are not, in most instances, our best thoughts: they are half-baked, poorly sculpted, underdeveloped.

Only through actual writing—moving sentences, adding imagery, adjusting syntax—do we arrive at what we really think . . . and thus, what we really want to say.

41.

When you're writing, it's rather like going on a very long walk, across valleys and mountains and things, and you get the first view of what you see and you write it down. Then you walk a bit further, maybe up onto the top of a hill, and you see something else. Then you write that and you go on like that, day after day, getting different views of the same landscape really.

The highest mountain on the walk is obviously the end of the book, because it's got to be the best view of all, when everything comes together and you can look back and see that everything you've done all ties up. But it's a very, very long, slow process.

~ROALD DAHL

MANY WRITERS hate to revise.

Lucky for me, I've never felt that way, nor have I ever truly understood why others would not jump at the chance to roll up their sleeves, dive right in, and improve what they have written.

Revision is my favorite part of writing, because I can look back from the highest of hills (the end of my latest draft) and see where I've been, where I wandered jaggedly off course, and where I might have saved myself some steps. Plus, it is at this point that I begin to have a sense of where I'm going (having just arrived).

Revision allows me to retrace my steps and adjust my journey, making it graceful and efficient, constructing the path I would have followed had I known all along where I was headed.

It can be a "very, very long, slow process," as Dahl suggests, but it is what writers do and it is worth every moment you spend.

42.

The greatest intensity in art in all its shapes is achieved with a deliberate, hard, and cool head.

~ TRUMAN CAPOTE

PASSION AND ENTHUSIASM can be useful in the beginning stages of any project, but that "deliberate, hard, and cool head" of which Capote speaks must come into play during revision, when you are slicing, erasing, rearranging, culling.

Be deliberate with each choice that you make, be hard on your own work, and exercise a surgeon's cool, firm disposition.

Or perhaps another way to put it would be to say:

Write with your passionate heart, but edit with your calm brain.

43.

My page one can end up a year later as page two hundred, if it's even still around.

~ PHILIP ROTH

THERE WAS A BOOK I wrote once—actually, I wrote it twice; two radically different versions, each revised numerous times. I put four years of my writing life into that book, churned out about 1,200 pages between the two versions—and the book never saw the light of day, except for a very small portion, an excerpt that I eventually published as an eight-page essay.

Wow, four years and 360,000 words, and that's all I ended up with?

Eight pages.

Yes. It happens sometimes.

Admittedly, that's an extraordinary ratio of words written to pages saved and not an experience I hope ever to repeat. But nothing I've written has ever escaped the basic reduction process—six pages drafted in order to find three good pages, or thirty pages in order to find a decent twelve.

The process of writing a book can easily entail a hundred pages of false starts, superfluous scenes, exploratory passages that were necessary for the writer to have written but *not* necessary for the reader to read in the end.

It is important to not become too attached to your opening chapter or opening page. Don't let yourself become stuck reworking the opening sentence for six hours before you allow yourself to move on to the rest of what you are writing.

That opening sentence may not even be there in the end.

44.

When we fall on the ground it hurts us, but we also need to rely on the ground to get back up.

~ KATHLEEN McDONALD

I HAVE LEARNED more from my failed stories, essays, and book projects over the years than I have ever learned from those works that came with relative ease. Failure teaches us valuable lessons:

Don't try that again.

Or try it a different way.

And those failures, now in my past, are the ground I use to get back up, when it seems I am failing again.

I have worked my way out of this narrative briar patch before, I tell myself, and with time and faith, I can work my way out of it again.

45.

Kill your darlings.

~WILLIAM FAULKNER

FAULKNER'S BLUNT admonition has made many a writer flinch.

Thankfully, Faulkner is talking about revision here, not actual murder. He is saying that we should stand ready to execute our sentences, our words, our images, our phrases, even if we love them dearly. It is easy to become attached to something because we have written it. We have given birth to it, it seems, and if not for us, this poem/story/essay would not exist.

But loyalty and unconditional love are best saved for your actual, flesh-and-blood progeny. Faulkner knows such devotion doesn't serve the writer *or* the writing.

Perhaps you have fallen in love with the sound of a certain sentence. Well, sometimes even a wonderful sentence has no place remaining in your work.

Kill your darlings.

Cutting is hard work, but necessary.

46.

**Language is a cracked kettle on which we
beat out tunes for bears to dance to,
while all the time we long to move
the stars to pity.**

~GUSTAVE FLAUBERT

WORDS WILL NEVER fully capture what is alive
in our hearts.

It would be a shame, though, if we denied the
bears their dancing.

So we thump our crude tunes on the side of
a cracked kettle.

It is what we do.

4

The Writer's Life

47.

**You will have to write and put away or
burn a lot of material before you are
comfortable in this medium. You might
as well start now and get the work done.**

~RAY BRADBURY

I MENTIONED EARLIER that there was a book
project I had worked on for four years, resulting in
the end in nothing more than an eight-page essay.

Here's the rest of that story:

Despite the interest of two publishers, and
the support of two excellent editors, the book
posed a storytelling problem that I simply could
not solve, no matter how much effort I poured
into it.

One July afternoon, I sat in my agent's office
in New York City, having driven into Manhattan
just for the day, so we could discuss the next
step with my stalled manuscript. "Why don't you
set it aside," she suggested after some mutual
hand-wringing. "Give the book a rest, and who

knows, maybe you will come back to it in a few years. Let's see what else you have to work on."

I wanted to throttle my agent right then and there, and I might have if I were not a believer in nonviolence (or if the receptionist had not been in such close hearing range). This had been years of hard work, and my agent wanted me to set it aside just like that?

I sputtered, she patted me down with consoling words, I sputtered some more, and left her office in a state of suppressed rage, shock, despondency, and confusion.

Thirty minutes later, though, as I headed home across the George Washington Bridge, I felt an unexpected high—as if the proverbial heavy load had been lifted from my shoulders. My agent was right after all. Despite the hard work, the soundness of my initial idea, the moments in the book that worked quite well (but not well enough to make the book complete or coherent), the project was making me unhappy, was likely to remain stalled for years to come, and my stubbornness to "finish what I had started" was sucking the life from my writing practice.

I was nearly whistling when I pulled into my Pennsylvania driveway four hours later, so sure that giving up on years of hard work was going to be the right action. The work, despite my efforts, had to be put away.

And it *was* the right action.

Within weeks, unexpected doors had opened.

By that autumn, I was writing a new book, the one, in fact, that I am proudest of so far in my career.

48.

For us there is only the trying.
The rest is not our business.

~ T. S. ELIOT

THERE IS A famous story in the Zen world:

> The student, newly arrived at the monastery, asks the master, "What work will I do as I seek enlightenment?"
>
> The master replies, "Chop wood, carry water."
>
> "And what work will I do once I achieve enlightenment?" asks the student.
>
> "Chop wood, carry water," replies the master.

How might that story apply to the writing life?

Well, consider for a moment the words "I am a writer." They convey an entirely different meaning from the words "I am someone who has written."

A writer writes. That's all there is to it. Occasionally she may care for her family, or she may put on a suit and work in an office. Sometimes a writer might go on the road and do readings or meet with a publisher to discuss marketing. A writer occasionally takes on a project where he is editing other people's work. Sometimes a writer stops to walk the dog, because the brown eyes have been pleading for hours.

But any writer, even a writer who has published a dozen books and won two dozen awards, gets up in the morning knowing what must be done. The words must be chopped and the sentences carried.

49.

Writing is a struggle against silence.

~CARLOS FUENTES

IT IS WISE to remind ourselves on occasion why we write, and why it matters so much. There is too much left unsaid in the world, either because what needs to be said is deemed impolite, because it is deemed dangerous, or because it contradicts the accepted version put forth by family, government, religious leaders, or the society we live in.

Fuentes knows that silence is as dangerous, perhaps more dangerous, than speaking out, and he knows that writing is one of the best ways we have of speaking out to a wide audience.

Not all writing is political or revolutionary, but the very act of giving yourself permission to write, to speak, to share the truth no matter whether the truth you understand is the truth others want to acknowledge, is brave, powerful, and important.

Remember that.

Remind yourself occasionally.
Be proud of what you do.

50.

I discovered that rejections are not altogether a bad thing. They teach a writer to rely on his own judgment and to say in his heart of hearts, "To hell with you."

~ SAUL BELLOW

I, FOR ONE, have never blamed editors for rejection. It hurts sometimes, disappoints almost all of the time, but I know that editing is a tough business. I try to be thankful that the editor put the effort into reading what I had submitted and agreed to share his or her professional judgment. I am not so vain as to think that every bit of writing I send out into the world is pure genius. And even if it were, different magazines have different needs.

Bellow is right, that sometimes the best reaction to a rejection note is "To hell with you." Take that poem, slap it into a fresh envelope, and send it along to another editor at another magazine.

But there comes the time when you have to stop and mindfully consider:

What does this rejection mean?

Maybe nothing more than a crowded slush pile, an editor who has different taste in literature, or an overworked intern, but perhaps it means the work is not as finished as you had imagined it to be the day you sent it forward. Maybe the images are not so clear.

Wishful thinking is a powerful force.

Don't allow yourself to become overly attached to the judgment of others. That, as Bellow warns us, can be a grave mistake.

But be mindful of your own wishful thinking.

If work is rejected time and again, there is a lesson to be learned there. Put on your reading glasses, pull up a chair, assume your most dispassionate pose, and read the rejected work slowly and with fresh eyes.

Chances are good that you'll see numerous ways to make it better.

51.

That's about as exciting a life as it is for a writer: You write sentences, and you cross out sentences.

~PAUL AUSTER

THIS QUOTE always makes me smile.

Many people want to be writers because they imagine it is a life of breezy cocktail parties, triumphant book tours, jovial fan mail, and endless champagne and caviar. Auster has known his share of success, but he also knows what it all comes down to:

Write a sentence.

Cross it out.

Write a better sentence.

52.

Your difficulties are not obstacles on the path, they are the path.

~EZRA BAYDA

HERE IS WHAT I tell myself on the days that I am blocked, on the days that I can write nothing, on the days that each new sentence I put down seems even more mundane than the last. I tell myself, "Don't worry, man, it is just a bad stretch you need to get through, and then you'll be okay for a while."

It helps me to think that I have a certain number of bad sentences stacked up inside of me (many, many bad sentences, I'm afraid), and they have to come out, like the dried glue often found at the tip of the tube; dried glue that has to be squeezed through the hole before you can access the good glue necessary to finish your current project.

That may have been one of my bad sentences right there. It sounds rather clunky. And this goofy glue metaphor may not be working at all.

But here is what I mean: If I have to squeeze those bad sentences out of my brain, out of my metaphorical writing tube, then I better get at it, better start squeezing.

With that logic, even the bad days are useful, even the obstacles are part of the path. Maybe I'm not writing anything worthy of preservation today, but if I am at my desk, writing, then I am making progress, because tomorrow the tube will be emptied of bad sentences, and the good stuff can finally flow out onto the page.

Or maybe none of that is true, really, and I am just tricking myself into staying at the desk.

But believing in this concept keeps me writing.

So I'm sticking with it.

53.

The writer's way is rough and lonely, and who would choose it while there are vacancies in more gracious professions, such as, say, cleaning ferryboats?

~DOROTHY PARKER

Writing is the hardest way of earning a living with the possible exception of wrestling alligators.

~WILLIAM SAROYAN

I LOVE A FUNNY METAPHOR.

To my mind, there are days that writing is like trying to mop the ferryboat's deck except the alligator keeps jumping up out of the muddy water and onto the boat. You have to wrestle that alligator. But all the wrestling just makes the deck grimy again. So you have to clean the deck once more. But—*Cripes Almighty!*—just then that alligator is back. So you wrestle for another few moments. And now a bit more mopping, because of the mess the two of you just made. And then the alligator returns, looking for some-one to grapple with . . .

On good days, the alligator gets tired before I do, and I finish my work.

On some days, the alligator and I just go on and on.

54.

Everyone thinks writers must know more about the inside of the human head, but that is wrong. They know less, that's why they write. Trying to find out what everyone else takes for granted.

~MARGARET ATWOOD

WHAT IS the single most important trait a writer must have?

People who ask that question often expect an answer such as good grammar, a wide vocabulary, or a comprehensive knowledge of the Greek and Roman classics.

But my answer:

Curiosity.

With curiosity, a writer will always move forward.

Without curiosity, the brain is already dead.

55.

Stay open, forever, so open it hurts, and then open up some more, until the day you die, world without end, amen.

~GEORGE SAUNDERS

WHAT EXACTLY does it mean to be open, all of the time?

Look at a child, maybe two years old, wide-eyed, full of wonder, amazed by the smallest thing—a yellow butterfly, a smooth rock, a stranger's smile—or, in an instant, ready to bawl at the world's pain and injustice.

Look at your average adult: jaded, seen-it-all, skeptical, ready to dismiss his own feelings as "false" because his intellect is trying to damp down the emotions.

The adult fellow I described above is me on most days, I'm afraid. But when I am writing, or should I say, when I am writing well, when I am in my "writing groove," I'm closer to that first person, the child fresh in the moment, surprised by everything, because I am seeing anew.

Living your life as a writer means regularly taking a self-assessment: Have you lost the wonder? Are you still insatiably curious about the world around you? Are you *feeling* as well as thinking? Are you able to see the rock, the butterfly, the smile, as if you were seeing it for the first time?

Are you still willing to bawl at all the world's injustice, to be so open that it actually does hurt?

56.

Yes, I've made a great deal of dough from my fiction, but I never set a single word down on paper with the thought of being paid for it . . . I have written because it fulfilled me. Maybe it paid off the mortgage on the house and got the kids through college, but those things were on the side—I did it for the buzz. I did it for the pure joy of the thing. And if you can do it for joy, you can do it forever.

~STEPHEN KING

IT IS GOOD to be reminded that writing is not just hard work, not just worrying about being blocked, not just struggle. Stephen King refers to the buzz of writing, that feeling of exhilaration that comes when the writing is flowing, streaming out like the tail end of a comet. That's the joy of it and the reason, I suppose, that we keep coming back.

Proper motives, what Buddhists call *right intention*, are easy to imagine and sometimes very hard to achieve. We are discontent creatures, the human race, and full of many deadly sins, or weaknesses at least. Perhaps that is why religions thrive and grow so powerful.

But Stephen King is offering us an important bit of wisdom here. Doing something—writing, for instance—not for money, not for fame, not for lording your achievements over others, but for the joy of it, the exhilaration, is not just the proper way to act, but it is what will best sustain you.

57.

To be fully alive, fully human, and completely awake is to be continually thrown out of the nest.

~PEMA CHÖDRÖN

AND ALONGSIDE that sense of joy, here is the other reason we keep writing: being constantly thrown out of the nest means being alive, feeling every moment of existence.

There are safer and easier ways to live your life than the incessant questioning that goes with being an honest writer, the constant challenging not just of other people's notions, but of your own. But those easier paths are often deadly dull, and with safety sometimes comes a series of confining boxes.

You have a choice—and your choices have consequences.

It is not always easy being continually thrown out of the comfortable nest, but it is far better than living your life in a box.

58.

You have to go to considerable trouble to live differently from the way the world wants you to live. That's what I've discovered about writing. The world doesn't want you to do a damn thing. If you wait till you got time to write a novel or time to write a story or time to read the hundred thousands of books you should have already read—if you wait for the time, you'll never do it. 'Cause there ain't no time; world don't want you to do that. World wants you to go to the zoo and eat cotton candy, preferably seven days a week.

~HARRY CREWS

THE WORLD does seem to conspire against the writer. Finding something to say and a fresh way in which to express it is difficult enough, surely, but add to that the low esteem in which writers are sometimes held, the problem of being taken seriously, and the difficulty can seem insurmountable.

Let's say your Aunt Bessie wants you to visit, and that visit is admittedly long overdue. If you pick up the phone and say, "Sorry Aunt Bessie, I love you, but I have to put new shingles on the garage roof this weekend," she might be disappointed, but she'll probably be understanding.

Tell her, on the other hand, that you have to stay home and work on your poems or stories, and unless Aunt Bessie is an uncommon supporter of the literary arts, you are likely to get something less than full approval. "You have to do what, dear? Are you sure?"

What a strange world where people will snicker at you for wanting to work on your writing for four hours but will often be totally accepting if you tell them you are planning to spend an entire day watching football on television.

As far as I'm concerned, you should be able to do either one, and people should accept your choices. Or you should be able to go to the zoo, and eat cotton candy, but only if you want to.

Frankly, I like football, hate cotton candy, and enjoy a good visit to the zoo. I also like Harry Crews' advice: Don't live your life the way the world wants you to live it. Live your life the way you want it to be lived.

And if the life you want includes writing, then don't wait for the permission.

That permission, most likely, will never come.

Except from yourself.

59.

**As a writer you are free. You are about
the freest person that ever was.
Your freedom is what you have bought
with your solitude, your loneliness.**

~URSULA K. LE GUIN

YES, WRITING IS TOUGH, but in the end it is well worth the effort. There is a freedom that comes from seeing clearly. There is a freedom that comes from cutting though illusion. There is freedom in no longer trying to control that which cannot be controlled.

We earn that freedom with the hard work of staying at our desk, struggling constantly to understand, searching for the perfect ordering of words and sentences, and working, working, and working, until we have created something that matters, something of which we are proud.

That's the pay-off.

That's why we do what we do.

Prompts for Mindful Writing

THESE PROMPTS are designed to help writers, beginning or experienced, to "see with fresh eyes," "hear with open ears," and "catch ourselves thinking." You might use them to find material to start a new poem, essay, or story, or you might use them to jumpstart a project that seems stalled, stale, lethargic.

Keep an open mind, always: if one of these prompts sends you off in a direction other than the prompt seems to be pointing, let go of "following rules" and trust your intuition. What bubbles up from parts unknown is almost always more valuable and alive than what we cobble together with our left-brained intellects.

The prompts can be attempted in any order,

and as many times as you wish. It is my hope that each attempt will bring new insight and a fresh glint of an idea.

And remember to breathe.

1. "Notice what you notice," Allen Ginsberg instructs us. As writers, poets, novelists, essayists, we have scripts inside of our heads suggesting what is suitable to write about, what is a "worthy" or "artistic" subject. Instead, grab your notebook, walk outside, and circle the block, or the field. Notice what you notice. Just log it in, without commentary. "I noticed that rock. I saw the way the sun glanced off of the tree limb." Then return to your writing space and study your list. What do the types of things that you notice say to you? About you? Write about it: in a poem, in an essay, or as if you were a character in a story. Follow your nose.

2. William Matthews reminds us, "The depth is

in the surface." Choose a moment in your life, somewhere in your past, that seems significant—for good or bad reasons—and write that moment down on the top of the page. Now, answer these questions, as honestly as you can (and, since no one will read these notes but you, why not be entirely honest?):

• What didn't I know at that moment in my life that I now know?

• What did I think I knew at that moment of my life, though it seems now I was probably wrong in my assumptions?

• What do I wish I had known then?

• What do I still not know?

• What will I never know?

Now, write about that moment, incorporating all of the unknowns.

3. Ginsberg also said, "Catch yourself thinking." It sounds so easy, but actually it is extremely hard, because once we become aware of our thoughts we start examining them, and suddenly we aren't thinking freely. Instead, we are thinking self-consciously and picking apart—probably judging—our thoughts. Keep a notebook in your pocket for three days, and practice writing down *what you were just thinking a moment ago*: the ideas and images that bubble to the top when you aren't paying attention. Again, write them down without commentary. "I was thinking about a tan rabbit I had seen next to the rose bushes this morning. I was thinking about the leftover pasta in the refrigerator." When you have accumulated forty or so thoughts, choose fifteen of them and make a list poem, or compose an essay, or put the thoughts in the mind of a fictional character, or whatever, but just follow your mind's lead.

4. "Don't tell me the moon is shining; show me the glint of light on broken glass," Anton Chekhov advised. Okay, what are three different ways of *showing* the reader that it is raining? That it is raining hard? That it is raining just a sheer, soft mist? What are three different ways of *showing* the reader that the air is still, but a storm is coming soon? What are three different ways of showing the reader that *you* (or perhaps a character you are writing) have a sore back? A sore heart? What are three different ways of *showing* the reader that someone is avoiding answering a question? What are three different ways of *showing* the reader that someone is very deeply in love?

5. Annie Dillard suggests, "Write as if you were dying." Let's take that seriously for a moment. If you knew you had only enough time left in your life to write one poem, one story, one essay, what would you write about? Why aren't you writing about it now?

Afterword

THE MESSAGE in this small book is simple enough:

First, don't grasp too hard or you will choke off any creativity.

Second, be open to the moment, the surprise, the gift of grace, or enlightenment.

If you are not mindful, not attentive, you will fall victim to the first and fail to recognize the second. So be alert. Be deliberate. Take care.

I am excited to see so many writers and artists echo these sentiments in the quotations gathered here because I know they are not speaking theoretically. The advice they offer is a reflection of hard-earned lessons, from individuals who have put in the time, the effort, and pieces of their own soul to come to some understanding. If this approach works for Flannery O'Connor, for

John Steinbeck, for Truman Capote, for Ursula Le Guin, then surely it must have value.

Let me close with one more reminder.

It is said that the writer Andre Dubus would end his writing session each day by marking down his word count. How many words had he managed in those four hours? After the number, whatever it was, he always wrote the words "thank you."

How wonderful that we have this maddening, beautiful, difficult, exhilarating, frustrating, mysterious, transformative ability to create worlds out of words.

What a gift. And what a challenge.

Write well, my fellow scribblers.

And thank you.

Index of Authors Quoted

About the Author

DINTY W. MOORE is a profes-
sor and director of creative writing
at Ohio University and is regularly
invited to speak and teach in the
US and Europe. In addition to publishing fiction
and nonfiction, he has published two books on the
art and craft of writing. He has been published in
Harper's, the *New York Times Magazine*, *Arts & Letters*,
the *Gettysburg Review*, *Utne Reader*, and many other
venues. He's also the author of *The Accidental Buddhist: Mindfulness, Enlightenment, and Sitting Still* and
is a National Endowment for the Arts fellowship
recipient.

Also Available from Wisdom Publications

Living Mindfully
At Home, at Work, and in the World
Deborah Schoeberlein David

"For everyone interested in bringing mindful awareness into their daily lives."—Susan Kaiser Greenland, author of *The Mindful Child*

Mindful Teaching and Teaching Mindfulness
A Guide for Anyone Who Teaches Anything
Deborah Schoeberlein David

"A gift for educators, helpful in any classroom, for any teacher and with every student."—Goldie Hawn, children's advocate and founder of the Hawn Foundation

Maya
A Novel
C. W. Huntington, Jr.

"I've been waiting for someone to write a contemporary 'quest for enlightenment' novel, but I didn't expect it to be this good."—David R. Loy, author of *A New Buddhist Path*

Sid
Anita Feng

"Anita Feng's book is mythical in spirit and light in tone, making it accessible for Buddhists and non-Buddhists alike. Sid's experience of enlightenment is a relevant one for an increasingly egocentric society; he does not become a famous teacher, but rather an individual who exudes curiosity and compassion for the world around him."—*Publishers Weekly*

About Wisdom Publications

Wisdom Publications is the leading publisher of classic and contemporary Buddhist books and practical works on mindfulness. To learn more about us or to explore our other books, please visit our website at wisdompubs.org or contact us at the address below.

Wisdom Publications
199 Elm Street
Somerville, MA 02144 USA

We are a 501(c)(3) organization, and donations in support of our mission are tax deductible.

Wisdom Publications is affiliated with the Foundation for the Preservation of the Mahayana Tradition (FPMT).